No Longer Bound

A STORY OF THE FATHER'S LOVE

JOEL AND LINDA BUDD

CROSSSTAFF
PUBLISHERS, LLC

Unless otherwise indicated, all Scripture quotations are taken from the *Holy Bible, New International Version. NIV*. Copyright © 1973, 1978, 1984, by International Bible Society. Used by permission of Zondervan Publishing House. All rights reserved.

Scripture quotations marked NKJV are taken from *The New King James Version* of the Bible. Copyright© 1979, 1980, 1982, 1983, 1984 by Thomas Nelson, Inc. Publishers. Used by permission.

No Longer Bound: A Story of the Father's Love
ISBN 10: 0-9743876-5-7
ISBN 13: 978-0-9743876-5-9
Copyright © 2007 by Joel and Linda Budd
1439 East 71st Street
Tulsa, OK 74136

Printed in the United States of America.
All rights reserved under International Copyright Law. Contents and/or cover may not be reproduced in whole or in part in any form without the express written consent of the Publisher.

"Hawaiians call it 'telling story.' Telling story is the sharing of life events. *No Longer Bound* is story, a very personal story! But it is not only story; it is also the spiritual lessons learned from an excruciating life event. Your heart will be touched as you read the story and your spirit will be encouraged as you ponder the rich biblical truths contained in *No Longer Bound*."

Paul L. Cox
Aslan's Place

"We are thrilled that Joel and Linda are so willing to share their healing and deliverance story with you. We pray you will be inspired and motivated to become whole and free as well. When we consider the extreme trauma they were subjected to by the medical, law enforcement, and human services personnel, it is surely a major outworking of Romans 8:28 that they did not become emotionally and spiritually crippled. Instead, they are tremendous examples of God's grace. They not only survived 'the vacation from hell,' but also they became stronger and more fruitful because of it. Today they are major instruments in the Lord's hands, bringing help, healing, and deliverance to many others. Thank You, Lord, for allowing us to be a part of their story."

Chester and Betsy Kylstra
Founders and Overseers
Restoring The Foundations Ministries

Dedication

To Joelle, our precious, beautiful daughter.

Acknowledgements

We want to thank all those who helped with our story, this book, and the spiritual and physical process behind it.

Thank you, Joelle, for having the courage and humility to let your story be told. Not only have you allowed the Holy Spirit to heal you, but you are allowing Him to use you to take vengeance on His enemies.

Thank you, precious daughters Cristin and Haley, for living through all of this story and more with us — and changing and getting healed with us.

Thank you, church family of Open Bible Fellowship. You have loved us, encouraged us, and empowered us to keep growing, keep changing, keep getting healed, and keep getting delivered. You have allowed the Holy Spirit to dig deep in you until He has created a healing atmosphere for us and countless others to come and be delivered, healed, and refreshed.

Thank you, John and Carol Arnott and the members of the Toronto Airport Church, for making a place for strangers like us to come and experience the Father's affection and the Holy Spirit's healing presence. At the most broken season of our lives we came among you and

God prepared a table before us. God's deep healing started for us on your floor.

Thank you, Dr. Paul and Donna Cox, for your consistently rich ministry at Aslan's Place, in our church, and in our home. God has used you in our lives and in this process of healing and deliverance.

Thank you, Dr. Chester and Betsy Kylstra. God used you to take us to some unhealed areas and bring another wave of restoration and deliverance. What you have done for us is being multiplied for many others.

Thank you, Scott Kaste, for patiently walking us through the process of getting this done. It literally would not have happened without you.

To Jeannie Cozad for all the transcribing, you added much to make this possible. Thank you and bless you.

Thank You, Holy Spirit, for being gracious to us and for giving us a new hunger and thirst for more of God when we didn't even know enough to be hungry. Your healing and blessing always go much deeper than any wounds. We testify to Your great ability to lead us, teach us, and heal us. You deliver us from evil.

Table of Contents

Foreword by Joelle Budd Burris 11

Foreword by John Arnott 13

Preface 17

Introduction 19

Chapter 1   A Word from the Lord 23

Chapter 2   My Brother's Keeper? 29

Chapter 3   The Enemy Strikes 33

Chapter 4   The Dark Night Begins 37

Chapter 5   Another Word from the Lord 43

Chapter 6   Not Business as Usual 47

Chapter 7   Never Really Alone 55

Chapter 8   The Dark Night of the Soul 65

Chapter 9   Understanding the Dark Night 75

Chapter 10 God's Purposes in the Dark Night 85

Chapter 11 How Other Believers May Respond ..93

Chapter 12 What Does God Want? 105

Chapter 13 Getting Delivered 117

Chapter 14 Where We Are Today 135

For Further Help... 140

About the Authors 141

Foreword

Because of the awesomeness of God I have been set free and am able to let this story be told. Not only has He healed me, but also He has healed my entire family. This book proves that in Jesus there isn't always just one victory but many victories after a tragedy.

I am so excited that the Holy Spirit and my parents have teamed up to create this book, which will be a tremendous weapon against the enemy. I believe our story and the revelation my parents received through it all will keep others from falling into Satan's traps. It will also be used by God to heal and deliver those who have had similar experiences as ours.

My prayer is that when you read our testimony and my parents' teaching, the Lord will visit you in a powerful way. If you too have gone through an experience in life that has left you bound and hurting, I believe after reading this book a new chapter of your life will begin — a chapter of joy and freedom you never dreamed possible.

Joelle Budd Burris

Foreword

I will never forget how shocked and surprised I was to hear Linda Budd share the depths of their family tragedy at a conference we were holding in Tulsa, Oklahoma. She said that the pain and the shame of it all nearly destroyed them, yet God came to their rescue.

As Christians and Christian leaders, most of us know that God is good and the devil is bad, but the stark reality of this truth remains mostly hypothetical until tragedy and adversity suddenly strike us and our families. We find ourselves plunged into the depths of the long dark night of the soul. Such is the testimony of Pastors Joel and Linda Budd. They were relatively successful pastors, fighting the good fight of faith, doing their best for the Lord and the kingdom of God, when suddenly they were caught up in the swirling nightmare of the rape of their four-year-old daughter.

Things quickly went from bad to worse as Joel, Linda, and their two little girls were roughly handled.

Joel and Linda were falsely accused and stranded with nowhere to turn. Although God supernaturally delivered them all, in the aftermath of that deliverance they desperately tried to hide the family's deep, dark secret. Eventually the inward pain and outward family bickering drove them to seek help — and the love of God found them. Flooded by the life-changing power of the Holy Spirit, the oppression and heaviness of the enemy began to break off. God's love took them step-by-step into His marvelous freedom.

If you or someone you know struggles with tragedy, pain, and disillusionment, this book is for you. The truth is, we are surrounded by people who have been beat up by the abuses and injustices of life. Too often these dear folks slip away into seething anger, fear, and shame, not knowing where to turn for help — or even if help exists.

This brave family was not content to merely receive the help they needed. They chose to share their story publicly with the whole world, knowing that help and freedom and hope would be given to many who are desperately looking for and needing

Foreword

ministry. As is usually the case, Joel and Linda received the healing love of God through various people in the body of Christ. Their desperation drove them to it. They faced their fears and were not disappointed. Neither will you be!

Begin to walk in the light with your shame, pain, and fear. Take God's hand and He will walk you out of that long, dark night of the soul. Freedom is there for you. As you face your fears with the boldness and faith that desperation often brings, you will discover that Romans 8:28 is true for you. "And we know that all things work together for good to those who love God (NKJV)."

This book will give you courage to walk into the light with your deep, dark secrets and be set free. God will provide a safe place for you too. Don't let your past continue to eat you alive. Deal with it. Take the freedom that God has for you. You have everything to gain and nothing to lose. You have a very big God who loves you!

John Arnott
Founding Pastor
Toronto Airport Christian Fellowship

Preface

If you have been a Christian for very long, you have probably heard some terrific messages. However, I want to warn you that the following message we are about to give is powerful on a very deep level. I believe one of the reasons it is so powerful is that it involves our personal story of one of the most traumatic events that can happen to a family, the rape of a child.

The first time Linda told our story was at our first women's conference. Over 250 women came from our church and most of them were delivered from terrible strongholds in a mighty way. Then she shared our message of healing from trauma at a conference, and I was astonished to see a large group of men set free along with the women. We discovered that this is a message for men and women of all ages. It hits a wound in the body of Christ that has been in need of healing for a long, long time.

We pray that as you read, you will be delivered of any trauma of the past you have endured. And if you know of someone who has been through a similar situation, please give them this book. Our mission is to see believers healed and whole and serving the Lord with peace and joy.

Introduction

Linda: It was a bright Saturday morning when I woke up from a deep sleep, sat up straight in bed, and yelled, "Shanakey!" Immediately I thought, *What in the world is that?* This happens to me from time to time, and when it does I know I have to do a little bit of research to find out what the Holy Spirit is saying to me. It took me about eight months of getting on the Internet and talking to people to discover the meaning of "shanakey," which is an Irish word that means "to tell a story."[1]

When I discovered the meaning of shanakey, the Lord said to me, "You have a story to tell, and now is the time to tell it. As you release it, it is going to unlock people from the pain of their past and terrible things that have happened to them. They will press in and experience the Father's heart and the Father's love in a deeper measure."

---

1 http://www.literarytraveler.com/print_tours.aspx?id=573

Telling a story of God's delivering power is a wonderful thing, but for various reasons many of us never tell what amazing things God has done for us in the midst of or in spite of terrible situations. For example, over twenty years ago, an older couple in our church told us a story that had happened to them. Their oldest daughter had gotten married, and in the first twenty-four hours of her honeymoon she found out he was a homosexual. She quickly had the marriage annulled and was totally brokenhearted. Later she married another man and had a happy family.

I asked this couple, "Why haven't you ever shared this story with anyone? It would help so many people to see that God is a good God, and He truly helps us get through terrible situations. We need to hear that from each other."

They answered, "Well, we just couldn't share this. We were so embarrassed and ashamed."

We want you to know that what we are going to share with you is not embarrassing to us. When God told me it was time to tell our story, I went to my family and said, "You know what, guys? I think now is the

Introduction

time for us to tell our family story." Then I specifically asked Joelle, "Are you ready for this?"

She said, "Yes, Mom. I would like you to begin telling this." We were all in agreement that the time was right, especially since Joelle had peace about it. You see, it was Joelle who had been brutally violated as a child.

We have no shame or guilt. Life happens, and we certainly didn't choose for this to happen in our family. It got dished out to us by the enemy. However, we learned from it. As we walked through this dark time in our lives we grew up in things like being sensitive to the leading of the Holy Spirit, trusting our Father's love for us, and putting all our faith in Jesus, our Deliverer and King.

The most important thing we learned was that God is always there for us in times of trouble, and He really does work all things together for our good (Romans 8:28). Every time we give our testimony other people get set free of the trauma of their past just like we did.

We encourage you to meditate on Psalm 20 as you read this book. Open up your heart to your Father and allow His love to heal all your wounds.

1 May the LORD answer you when you are in distress; may the name of the God of Jacob protect you.

2 May he send you help from the sanctuary and grant you support from Zion.

3 May he remember all your sacrifices and accept your burnt offerings. Selah

4 May he give you the desire of your heart and make all your plans succeed.

5 We will shout for joy when you are victorious and will lift up our banners in the name of our God. May the LORD grant all your requests.

6 Now I know that the LORD saves his anointed; he answers him from his holy heaven with the saving power of his right hand.

7 Some trust in chariots and some in horses, but we trust in the name of the LORD our God.

8 They are brought to their knees and fall, but we rise up and stand firm.

9 O LORD, save the king! Answer us when we call!

Psalm 20

CHAPTER 1

A Word from the Lord

Linda: The year was 1985. Joel and I had been pastoring our church for about two years, and it was going pretty well. We had close to four hundred members by then. My brother and his first wife lived in Arizona, and they kept calling and asking, "Why don't you take a break and come down for Christmas? We would just love to see you! And wouldn't it be fun to take Cristin and Joelle (our third daughter had not been born yet) and our two girls, jump in our van, and drive to Disneyland for New Year's Eve?"

We thought that sounded like a great idea! We didn't have much money and really weren't sure if the church was healthy enough for us to leave at that time, but we finally said, "Let's do it!"

During the Sunday service before we were to leave, a lady we had never seen before came with someone who was well-known in the church. At the close of the service she walked up to me and said, "I have a prophetic word for you. It's actually not just for you, but it's for you and your husband and for this church. I know that you don't know me, but can I give this to you?"

At that time we didn't know anything about the prophetic. We were not moving like that. We were really an evangelical type of church, although we called ourselves a charismatic church. I was not comfortable with this whole prophecy thing, but I was curious. I said to her, "Well, you know, let me get my husband because I don't want to do this by myself. And let me get an elder because I think that would be good." She respected that and was grateful for my boundaries, so it wasn't a problem.

With Joel and an elder beside me, she gave us the following word. "This church is going to become very powerful. I see the Lord using your family as a sacrifice poured out over the church. It's going to create a brokenness in you that is going to lead to the healing of many. The church is going to be very strong and very powerful, but your family is going to be used as a sacrifice for that to happen."

As I had never had a prophetic word given to me before, this one scared the heebie-jeebies right out of me! I didn't know what it all meant, but it didn't sound too good. I thought, *You want to be poured out like a sacrifice over a bunch of people you're not even sure you like yet? And what does that mean anyway?* Even so, I immediately knew that something was up.

By this time I was thirty years old and had been a Christian for fifteen years. I didn't know a whole lot about the power and gifts of the Holy Spirit, but I had been saved a long time. Looking back, I see how I had lived all that time in the shallow end of the pool — and that makes you a prime target for the enemy. I had just enough of Jesus and His anointing working in me to attract the opposition of the devil and his demons but not enough knowledge to fight and protect myself in warfare.

I was doing all the Martha stuff in the church and neglecting the Mary stuff. I didn't have any idea how the Holy Spirit moved in the gifts or in power. My experience and knowledge of prophecy was just barely limited to the understanding that the prophetic is supposed to be for edification, comfort, and exhortation. I had no clue that the Holy Spirit could move someone in the prophetic realm to actually warn you about things that are going to happen.

Needless to say, I was confused at this word from the Lord, and so I put it on the back burner. I thought, *We're going to leave tomorrow for this trip. I don't know what this is all about. This scares me, but let's just shut that down for a little bit.*

As we were getting ready, however, we had no peace inside. We felt all kinds of turmoil, and we should have just said, "No. We can't do this." But sometimes when you're young or you have a lot of selfishness going on in you, you won't listen to the Spirit of the Lord. You won't care about the fact that there's no peace. You just want what you want. And I wanted to go see my family and go to Disneyland. I had grown up on the farm, we had lived in poverty, and all my life I had dreamed about going to Disneyland. All I could think was, *Wow! What a great opportunity. And I get to take my kids!*

My selfish desire ruled out the warnings of the Holy Spirit inside me, and I chose to ignore all the turmoil. I should have stopped to pray and seek His mind and will before doing anything, but I didn't know to do that in those days. I didn't know you are supposed to pray and ask God about it when someone gives you a word from the Lord. I didn't know what prophetic intercession was. I didn't know what it meant to war in the Spirit when He was telling you something bad was about to happen so that the strategies of the enemy could be exposed and undone. All I knew was that I wanted to go to Disneyland with my family.

Knowing what we know now, of course, if we had to do it all over again we would never have gone on that trip. But we went anyway. On the drive to Phoenix I turned to Joel and said, "You know that prophetic word that we got yesterday? That *really* scared me."

He said, "You know what? It scared me too."

I said, "Well, I feel like I know it's about Joelle." I wasn't trained in the prophetic, but that didn't mean the Holy Spirit wasn't talking to me. Inside I just felt like I knew that word was about Joelle. She had just turned four the previous month. I said, "I'm really afraid."

Joel grabbed my hand and said, "You know what? This doesn't happen to me either, but when that word came to us, I got a picture of Joelle. I felt it was about her too."

I began crying because Joel's words hadn't given me any comfort. Then he prayed a nice little prayer like, "Jesus, would You just protect our daughter. We don't understand what this is all about, but just help us."

And we still kept moving toward Arizona and Disneyland.

CHAPTER 2

My Brother's Keeper?

We arrived at my brother's house in Phoenix and were not welcomed with warm fuzzies like we expected, especially after they had begged us to come for months and months. Instead, we were ignored. Joel and I just looked at each other, thinking, *What's going on here?*

My brother's wife, who is now his ex-wife, didn't want anything to do with us. We thought maybe she was overwhelmed because she had a house full of people. We just tried to be nice and somehow got through the Christmas dinner, which also wasn't very warm and fuzzy.

We were relieved when it was time to leave to go to Disneyland. We all got in their big van and were driving along when little Joelle got hungry and wanted a cracker. I started to get one out for her and my sister-in-law went bonkers. "You're not going to have that in my van and mess it up! Put that away!"

I said, "Okay. Then can you pull over? She really needs something to eat."

"No, we can't do that, either. We need to get to Disneyland."

I didn't back down, and they eventually pulled over. By this time I had had it. I turned to my brother's wife and said, "What's bothering you? What's really on your heart? What's going on here?" In Matthew 5:23-24 Jesus said, "Therefore, if you are offering your gift at the altar and there remember that your brother has something against you, leave your gift there in front of the altar. First go and be reconciled to your brother; then come and offer your gift." So that's what I tried to do with my sister-in-law.

She proceeded to tell me how all these years she had hated me because she knew that I did not want her to marry my brother. I had never told her that, but before they were married I had seen things in her that were not right. I believed it would never work out, and I told my brother that. That was the prophetic working in me whether I knew it or not, trying to warn my brother, and it was the truth because later they were divorced. Unfortunately, he told her what I had said, and she had held that offense against me all these years.

I said to her, "Would you please forgive me for that? That was a long time ago. We were all teenagers."

She said, "No. I can't forgive you."

With that we just got back in the van and continued on to Disneyland. There's nothing more important, you know, than Mickey Mouse and Donald Duck!

We got to Disneyland late in the day and checked into a Motel 6 that seemed to be a really nice one. There was a nice outdoor pool with a garden area, and the rooms were in real good condition. We ran over to Disneyland to spend the evening and enjoy it a little bit, but for the next few days both of my kids began taking turns getting sick. Between their not feeling well and my sister-in-law's determination to make us as miserable as possible, by the 30th of December (and I'm naming this day because it's important) we were ready to go home. We didn't care that New Year's Eve was the next day, and we were going to miss all the fun. We had had enough "fun." Even my brother had had enough. He couldn't stand the way his wife was acting.

We said, "Can we just go home?"

Everybody said, "Yes!"

CHAPTER 3

The Enemy Strikes

While we packed our stuff in our rooms, which were on the ground floor, our door was open, the window curtains were pulled back, and we could see our four little girls outside. They were playing together and running around the swimming pool and garden area. There was no danger for them under our watchful eyes. As soon as we were packed someone suggested we go to Denny's and get some breakfast, which we did.

After breakfast we got in the van to drive back to Phoenix, but Joelle would not get in her car seat. She always loved her car seat, so this was really odd. In fact, she was acting really strange. She kept crawling under the seats of the van, hiding. Finally I pulled her out, spanked her for not obeying me, and said, "Get in your seat *now*."

She got in her seat, but I could tell that she was not herself. I thought she was just tired from all the stress of the trip and the tension between the adults. Children always sense that stuff. After a long time of driving we stopped to use the restroom. Joelle didn't go to the bathroom, and when I asked her to go she didn't want to. I realized it had been five hours since she had gone last.

That night we stayed at a hotel on the road, and Joelle finally went to the bathroom. I noticed there was blood in her urine. This really scared me because I knew that could mean something terrible was wrong with her. No wonder she had been acting strangely! I thought she must have a kidney infection because she had been sick and on antibiotics. But by the time we got to Phoenix the next day, there was a steady flow of blood coming out of her and she looked bad.

We asked my brother and his wife, "Would you please help us to find a hospital? We need to go right now."

My sister-in-law said, "No. We will not help you." Then she turned to my brother and said, "It's time for you to choose. You pick her or you pick me. It's one or the other, but it's not both of us." He stood there, totally dumbfounded, not knowing what to do. We could see the look of shock on his face, and finally he said, "Well, I have got to pick my wife."

We said, "We understand. Can you please help us, though? Our daughter's in trouble and we don't know Phoenix. We don't know where the nearest hospital is. Can you please take us?"

"No, I can't."

"Will you tell us where it is?" So he did, and we got in our car and rushed to the hospital. We went straight to the emergency room and told the doctors Joelle had blood in her urine and probably had a bad kidney infection, but we didn't know for sure. They whisked her into the examining room, and she was scared and screaming for us, which was also not like her. She wouldn't stay still for them to examine her and didn't want them to look at her bottom, so I had to restrain her and hold her down. Once they got a good look they sent me to the waiting room, where Joel was taking care of Cristin, who was seven.

Soon a doctor came and told all three of us to follow him. He took us to a private waiting room, where we really got worried that something terrible was wrong with Joelle. All of a sudden a policeman came in and they turned on us. They were extremely angry with us and said, "We found semen in your daughter's body. She has been raped."

CHAPTER 4

The Dark Night Begins

Joel and I were in *absolute shock*. Never in our wildest dreams had we thought of something like rape. The policeman asked, "Who did this?" and, of course, we had no idea.

We said, "This can't have happened. We were on a family vacation. We were together all of the time. This could not have happened."

The doctor said, "We have proof that she has been raped. Someone did this to her."

Then we found out that when the authorities don't know who raped your child they blame the daddy. They took Cristin and me to another room in the hospital that was tiny and dark, and they put us in there by ourselves. We didn't know where they took Joel, and when I had asked how Joelle was they wouldn't tell me. They acted like she was no longer my child.

Next, they brought a detective in the room to talk with me. At first he was very nice and told me how sorry he was that this had happened. Then a few minutes later he took Cristin and me to another room where he began yelling at us and saying the most horrific things — things I will never repeat — and my seven-year-old daughter had to hear them. Basically he accused me of setting up the rape and allowing Joel to rape our daughter in order to please him.

If I had been in shock before, now I was completely demoralized. After going through a horrendous "vacation" with my brother's wife, having to see my brother choose between me and his wife, realizing that my precious daughter was bleeding, being told that she had been brutally raped — now they were accusing Joel and me of hurting her, whom we loved so much. My emotions were raw. I felt like someone had died, and yet no one had.

I tried desperately to make them understand that there was no way Joel would ever do what they were accusing him of doing. No matter how they screamed and threatened, I refused to say anything but, "Absolutely not! This man would never do anything like this. You've got this all wrong. I don't know who did this, but he did not do it."

The interrogation went on and on from room to room, and Cristin witnessed every part of it. They were nice one minute and angry the next, trying to "break me down" I guess. But all I could say was the truth: I didn't know what had happened, but Joel was innocent. At one point my legs turned to jelly and I started to faint, but I caught myself in midair. The detective just laughed at me.

After several hours of this, they took us to another room. That's when we saw Joel in the hallway. We began to go to each other when two policemen got out their clubs and acted like they were going to beat him if he took another step. At this Cristin became hysterical and began screaming, "Daddy! Daddy!"

Joel said, "I did not do this," and backed up against the wall. The policemen were still holding their clubs over him, and I was horrified. Afraid of what might happen, I held Cristin back from going to Joel.

After this incident Cristin and I were separated from Joel again. I was worried about him, but I was worried sick about Joelle. They wouldn't tell me anything about her condition. My heart cried out to God, "Help me!"

At one o'clock in the morning they told me that they were taking Joelle someplace where we could not find her. At that moment all I could think about was how she must be feeling. She knew she had been violated. She probably didn't understand it and blamed herself because that is what kids do. And I knew she was afraid and alone. My heart was breaking, but I did what I believed was the only thing I could do to help her. I said, "Well, if you're going to take her, then you have to take this one too. I don't want Joelle to think that I've abandoned her because she did something bad. So you have to take Cristin too. She will protect her sister."

I hugged Cristin and explained that she was going to be with Joelle and help Joelle until her daddy and I could get there. The authorities were glad to take her.

The Dark Night Begins

Then I was alone for a while, hardly able to wrap my brain around what had just happened to our family, wondering if God was anywhere in this mess.

All of a sudden they released Joel to me. They practically kicked us out of the hospital, giving us a phone number and saying, "It's a holiday, so in three days you can call this number and you might get some answers." It was New Year's Eve, in the middle of the night, every hotel and motel we tried was full, and we could not go back to my brother's house. We finally found a vacancy in a hotel, which was probably in the worst part of Phoenix. Cockroaches had free run of our room.

Joel and I collapsed on the bed, and Joel drifted off to sleep while I laid there in shock. I finally got up, went into the bathroom, shut the door, turned on the lights, and sat down. I didn't think there were any tears left, but I began to sob.

CHAPTER 5

Another Word from the Lord

If I had been a smart woman of the Word during this crisis, sitting in the bathroom that early morning of New Year's Eve, I might have remembered the story in 1 Kings 3:16-28. This story is told in the Bible as an example of King Solomon's wisdom. Two mothers were fighting over the same child. Both claimed to be the child's mother, and no one could determine who was telling the truth. They brought the case to King Solomon, who asked for a sword and said, "Okay, we'll cut this child in half."

At that moment the real mother came forward and said, "No! Give the child to that other woman." Solomon knew that the real mother was the one who would rather give up her child than see the child killed. Without realizing it, the Holy Spirit had given me the wisdom to give up Cristin so Joelle would not be alone, and if I had remembered the story of the two mothers in the Bible, I would have known that God was going to come through for us. But I wasn't a woman of the Word, I had little understanding of the operations of the Holy Spirit, and I was filled with fear and hopelessness and defeat. I didn't feel any faith whatsoever. I just wanted to die. So I sat in the bathroom and cried out to God, which was all I knew to do.

Then something miraculous occurred. The Lord told me what had happened to Joelle. He said, "In the few minutes that you were putting stuff in the car, getting ready to leave the hotel, the kids were not in the pool but were playing near it. A twelve-year-old boy approached Joelle and told her that if she didn't let him do what he wanted, he was going to drown her."

I bolted out of the bathroom to wake up Joel. I told him what the Lord had said to me. He looked at me questioningly and asked, "How do you know?"

I said, "The Lord just told me."

Another Word from the Lord

From that moment all we could think about was that we had to wait two days — an eternity — before we could dial the phone number they had given us and try to get Joelle and Cristin back. We held onto each other and Joel fell back to sleep. I tried to sleep but the fear and the tears wouldn't stop.

As soon as we got up the next morning, we called the elders of our church. One of them traveled to Phoenix because she knew how to work with the Department of Human Services (DHS). She had done this kind of work in Tulsa. She graciously sat with us in that horrible hotel for the remaining two days. When the holiday was over, she began calling and calling until she finally got through to someone. She told them that I knew what had happened to Joelle, and they agreed to see us.

We went to the DHS offices and sat down across from a woman. Before she could make any accusations or say anything, I said, "I don't know if you're a Christian, but I'm a Christian. And I did not know what had happened before, but the Lord spoke to me two days ago, and this is what He told me."

As I related exactly what Jesus had said to me, she began to smile. When I finished she said, "We could not get Joelle to talk to us because she was so afraid, but she whispered something to Cristin. Cristin then told us what Joelle said to her. What you just said were the exact words Joelle whispered into her sister's ear. And because the child is saying it and you're saying it, there's nothing we can do to hold the girls any longer." Then she handed us an address where we could go to pick them up.

We were relieved that they had been placed in a nice, residential area in Phoenix, a DHS safe house. But when we walked into the house, the place was a disaster. Cristin and Joelle came running to our arms looking ragged, like they hadn't had a bath for three days. Their hair was matted, and they were both sick. I said, "Let's get out of here and never come back." For years I couldn't go back to Phoenix.

CHAPTER 6

Not Business as Usual

When we got home our elders counseled us not to tell anyone what had happened. They said, "Joelle can decide whether she wants this known or not when she's an adult." We thought that sounded good, like we were protecting her, so we decided to not talk about it and go on with our lives as though nothing had happened. The elders also prayed that Joelle would have no memory of the rape, that she would not be affected by it in any way.

There was only one problem. I was someone who told everything about herself and didn't know how to hide anything. Therefore, it was really hard for me not to talk about this for all those years. All the pain was bottled up inside me, and we began to have marriage problems. Joel and I were fighting all of the time. We knew we loved each other, but we couldn't stop fighting. And it was never about anything important.

Our relationship got bad enough that we decided we needed to see a counselor. The very first thing he said to us after he heard how we were treating each other was, "And you guys call yourselves Christians? And you guys pastor a church? Ha! Ha!" He made fun of us, and I couldn't handle it. I did not need one more person causing me shame. I didn't want to go back to him, but I tried two or three more times before I refused to see him again.

For five more years we suffered in our marriage. It was *bad*. Then we decided to go to a conference at John Wimber's church in California. At this time in my life I rarely talked to God, but on the flight out there I told Him, "If You don't help me with this marriage, I can't do this any longer." Then I heard a person's name in my spirit. I thought, *Well, that's interesting.*

We stayed with a great friend of mine who had previously lived in Tulsa. As soon as we had a minute alone, I told her how Joel and I had been fighting all the time, that I had told the Lord I was giving Him one more chance to "fix" us, and He had given me this name. My friend started laughing and said, "I know who that is. He's a Christian marriage counselor and therapist in Tulsa, and he's absolutely great. That's who I was going to tell you to go to."

I was astonished. It seemed God was still interested in us! You may be thinking, *She's a pastor of a church and she's surprised God is interested in her family?* But that was where I was spiritually. As I have said before, even though we were pastoring a growing church we were really shallow in our spiritual lives. Most of the time when I read the Bible I was frustrated because it said we were supposed to do the stuff Jesus did and we weren't. I didn't know where to begin to do what Jesus did except tell people about Him and lead them to Him — and we were not doing much of that either. It is important that you understand this because it has a lot to do with how God delivered us from the trauma of Joelle's rape.

As soon as we returned to Tulsa we made an appointment with the counselor both the Lord and my friend had told me about. From the first session we had with him things began to get better. We told him all our stuff except the incident with Joelle. I told him about my horrific background, and Joel began to share some of the dysfunctional stuff he had grown up with. We found out that we didn't know how to communicate with each other the right way. We had to change the way we talked to each other, listened to each other, and responded to each other.

We got so much better that we taught our kids what we were learning. Then we shared our testimony (just about our marriage problems being healed) and brought our counselor in to talk to our congregation. We encouraged couples who were having problems to get help and told them it was the best money we had spent in years.

Now Joel and I could communicate, but that didn't make the pain go away. It just allowed us to talk to each other more honestly and eventually tackle the pain together. Despite the improvement in our marriage, I was still dying inside and Joel was frustrated and crying out to God, "Fill me or kill me!" I was depressed, discouraged, and exhausted all the time — and I didn't know why. There was a heaviness that pressed on me continuously. Then one day a friend called Joel and told him about unusual meetings in Toronto, at a church near the airport. When Joel told me about it, we agreed we needed to go right away. Both of us were desperate for something. We didn't know what.

We talk about what happened next in our book, *Fill Me or Kill Me*, in great detail; but when we attended that conference at the Toronto Airport Christian Fellowship, God met us there and we have never been the same. Our friend had said to Joel, "I cannot explain it to you, but you must go there. Those people get up early in the morning, and they just start seeking God. Then He just comes all over them, and they lay out on the floor all day long and almost all night until two o'clock in the morning. Everybody goes home, gets a little sleep, and then they come back and do it all over again." Our friend didn't exaggerate! And it was exactly what we needed.

The power of God came on me so strongly during our time in Toronto that I was laid out on the floor and began to shake. As I lay on the floor, I had visions of

Jesus telling me that I was the best thing He ever made. He loved that I was a girl, and He delighted in me. He loved my name and everything about me. We played together and laughed together. And somewhere in the course of all that, all of the pain and shame of my child being raped began to flow out of me.

Nothing like that had ever happened to me before. I had never even heard of this happening to Christians. I shook almost constantly for two years as Jesus delivered me from the trauma and healed all the wounds of my past. He just shook all the pain, the demonic voices, the condemnation, and all the shame right out of me.

Every day I felt better. Little by little the depression and heaviness that had been pressing on me left. I started feeling so happy and free. All of a sudden the fact that Joelle had been raped almost while we were watching her, that Joel and I had been falsely accused and horribly interrogated, and that my children had been ripped from me didn't affect me at all. There was no more pain, shame, or bitterness attached to it because *Jesus was everything to me now and He loved me!*

He loved me and cherished me despite all my past and human faults and weaknesses!

Joelle is now in her twenties and is a healthy, wonderful, happily married young woman. The reason she is not talking about this herself is because she doesn't remember it at all! When the elders had prayed for her not to remember, I thought it would be a bad thing, but now I believe differently. To this day she has absolutely no memory of it. If we talk about it, to her it's like we're talking about a different family. We've taken her to a counselor and tried all kinds of things to dig it up, but it's just not there because God erased it.

We're a family who has walked through a terrible trauma and has been powerfully delivered by our loving heavenly Father. His love gave us our lives back with greater joy and understanding than we could ever have imagined before all this happened. We learned so much about our Father and how He helps us and delivers us when we live through terrible things in life. That's what Joel is going to talk about in the next few chapters as he shares his side of our story. If you've been through trauma and have a lot of pain in your life, I promise you that you will be blessed by what he is going to share with you.

CHAPTER 7

Never Really Alone

Joel: At some point during the long wait at the hospital emergency room I remember being told the doctor would like to talk to us about Joelle. We were ushered to a small family conference room. I was surprised at the number of staff already present. The doctor was seated and a policeman was there.

The moment we walked into the room the doctor began to speak in a cold and angry tone, telling us that Joelle had a bladder or kidney infection. Then he lifted his head, glared at me with contempt, and said, "When we examined your daughter we found semen in her vagina."

His words didn't register. I couldn't connect these last words with the first words about bladder infection. I heard Linda say, "What does that mean?"

The doctor's anger seemed to double, if that was possible. "It means," he said staring angrily at me, "someone has tried to have intercourse with your daughter." Before either of us had a chance to say another word he immediately began to walk to the door, saying, "There are some people here who are going to want to ask you some questions and take your statements." Then he and his staff left in silence.

Immediately the police officer turned to me and said, "I want you to stay here. We will be right back." He asked Linda and Cristin to follow him, leaving me alone and in shock. I remained standing because he said he would be right back, but no one came right back. Finally I sat down and began to pray, crying a little, expecting the police and Linda any moment. They never came.

I replayed the scene with the doctor in my mind. I began to wonder why he was so angry at me. Although in shock and disbelief I began to process what had just happened. I thought, *The doctor was angry at me because he thinks we are negligent, or worse, he thinks I did it! Where's Linda? Why have they been gone so long?*

They must be taking her statement without me! The longer I waited and processed the more the unthinkable began to present itself: *These people think I raped my little daughter.*

Then I told myself, "Don't even worry about it. That's absurd! Innocent people have nothing to fear." Nevertheless, I was beginning to feel afraid for Linda, for me, and for Joelle. For the hour or so that I was alone, I began to wonder if I was *locked* in this little conference room. After awhile I checked the door and found it unlocked. I stepped outside and stood in the hallway. I waited some more. I began walking up and down the hallway in front of my "cell."

Just a little way down the hall was the emergency room waiting area. I heard the television in there and realized the ball was about to drop in Times Square...a new year was about to begin. I thought, *Yeah! Happy New Year! You bet! This is unbelievable! It's New Year's Eve and I'm in a strange town, in an emergency room because my daughter is sick. And now they tell me she has been raped. I don't know where she is, and my wife is who knows where. Are they treating Linda like they are treating me, or are they with her, questioning her? Is she with Joelle? Is Joelle alone? She was so scared!*

I began to pray in the Spirit. The longer I prayed the more the frozen emotions began to thaw and the shock began to wear off. I was still afraid, so I prayed more, harder and more aggressively. I walked into the ER waiting room, which was empty, still praying in the Spirit. The only other person visible was Dick Clark in Times Square. The ball dropped. I didn't care. I just kept praying, crying, and praying some more.

As I glanced at the clock at 12:40 A.M., I realized my mood had begun to change. I didn't feel frozen anymore. I didn't feel quite as helpless and compliant. Praying in the Spirit was affecting the shock and fear and unbelief. I started thinking more clearly and started thinking more about Joelle. *Where is she? What are they doing with her? Is that angry doctor with her? She needs love and comfort not that angry man!* I thought, *It doesn't matter what they think about me! I'm Joelle's dad and I'm going to find her and be with her and help her!*

I went back towards the hallway. The sign said, "Authorized Personnel Only." I thought, *That's me! I'm*

Joelle's dad. No more sitting around scared. I'm going to be with Joelle.

I entered the hallway and walked past exam rooms, hearing the tired cries of a little girl. I found the room and looked around the corner. There was little Joelle on an examination table with two nurses and a doctor. I heard them telling her that they needed to examine her again. As the doctor moved toward her feet she started to scream and kick. The nurses tried to hold her down, but she was fighting like a little tiger, kicking and screaming in terror.

Before I thought about it I was in the room, next to her, saying, "It's okay, Honey! Daddy's here. Daddy's here. Look at me." She was almost hysterical, her eyes filled with fear. I took her face in my hands and told her to look at me. She stopped screaming at once.

I could hear the medical staff talking as I rubbed Joelle's forehead and spoke softly to her. They said, "I don't think he's supposed to be here." I responded to them by talking to Joelle, just inches from her face. "Honey, you don't have to be afraid. Daddy's here. They need to touch you to help you. They are not being naughty to you; they are here to help you. I'll hold you and be with you."

She calmed down but was still crying and scared. I told the staff, "I'm her dad and I'm here to help her. The only way you are going to get this done is if I'm here. I'll hold her, and you do what you need to do to help her."

I could be wrong, but I sensed they were watching to see if Joelle was better or worse with me being in the room. She wasn't afraid of me. She responded to me and trusted me. I was not the "bad man," and she wasn't afraid of me.

With Joelle crying and me holding her, what probably should have been the most horrible experience of my life began to change. God's grace came over me. I felt His strength and His courage. I think He helped me to be strong for her. I tried to talk her through it and love her through it. I knew I had no strength to do what I was doing. Only God could be doing it. But I was there — and so grateful Joelle wasn't alone.

After the examination a man introduced himself to me as a detective and asked me to step out in the hall. Linda and Cristin were there with a policeman. The detective said, "Let me tell you what's going to happen next." He began to walk down the hall, so I walked alongside him.

The policeman and Linda and Cristin were right behind as we walked toward the ER waiting room. Without looking at me he said, "What's going to happen next is we are going to take your two daughters into protective custody. We will turn them over to DHS and put them in a safe house for a few days while we continue our investigation."

I said in a clear, firm, calm voice, "No. You aren't taking them anywhere. These are my daughters and they are staying with us. They have been through enough and they need…" Before I finished the sentence the detective grabbed me by the collar with both hands and violently threw me back against the wall. My head hit the wall and the sudden, violent action jarred and shocked me. He had his arm pressed against my throat and was pushing against my chest with his other hand.

His hate-filled face was about three inches from mine, and a demonic voice seethed, "You listen to me, preacher! You have no say in this matter!"

Suddenly standing next to me was the uniformed policeman with his night stick drawn and raised. I heard little Cristin screaming, "Don't hurt my daddy! Don't hurt my daddy!" Because I had done nothing to provoke this excessive, abusive use of force, I knew I had just undergone a physical, demonic attack through the detective.

As suddenly as he had attacked me, the savage, demonic voice was gone and the nice, calm detective voice was back. "Now I'm going to let go, and you aren't going to give me any trouble, are you?" I nodded my head. He let go and acted like none of it had happened. The "nice" detective began to explain what normal procedure was in a case like this, and he gave us the telephone number of the case worker the girls would be assigned to.

When I asked why they had to take Joelle away, he told me I was the prime suspect. I assured him he was wrong and volunteered to take a lie detector test. I said,

"Let's settle this here and now. I'll take a lie detector test. I'll cooperate 100 percent. I have nothing to hide." The next thing I knew the girls were gone and Linda and I were ushered out of the hospital. The only connection we had to our precious girls was a little piece of paper with a telephone number on it.

CHAPTER 8

The Dark Night of the Soul

It isn't hard to understand that when Linda, our girls, and I went through the harrowing experience of Joelle being raped, we entered a time many Christians through the ages have called "the dark night of the soul." This is a time when we wonder if God forgot our names, lost our address, and if, when we cried out, He either put us on hold or ignored us.

Our relationship with Jesus is a love relationship because He is God and God is love. That is why the dark night of the soul is so baffling, frustrating, and emotionally painful. For some reason that we cannot explain, we believe Jesus has backed away from us and is no longer showering us with His love and blessings — usually when we are facing a terrible situation. We cannot reconcile the experience we are having with the fact that in Matthew 28:20 He promised to be with us always and forever.

I believe the experience of the dark night of the soul is why the Holy Spirit put the Song of Songs in the Bible. The whole book is about the ups and downs of a love relationship. King Solomon is in love with the Shunammite woman, and she is in love with him. Solomon is a type of Jesus, who is our King and the lover of our souls; and the Shunammite woman is a type of His bride, the Church, who loves and worships Him. If we read Song of Songs and see King Solomon as King Jesus and the Shunammite woman as ourselves, we gain great insight into our love relationship with the Lord and what He seeks to accomplish through the dark night of the soul.

Fainting for Love

I slept but my heart was awake....

Song of Songs 5:2

In this verse the Shunammite woman is saying she had such peace with God in her spirit that she slept, but her heart was alert to any sound of the approach of her king and lover. Her love was so intense that even when she was sleeping peacefully, her heart was listening for the sound of his footsteps. She did not want to miss a moment she could spend with him, and she could not get enough of him.

A.W. Tozer called this the paradox of love, which is to have discovered the great depths of Jesus' love in an intimate relationship with Him and yet to continuously desire more of Him. It is not the dissatisfaction we felt as unbelievers, which is motivated by self-gratification. This desire for the Lord is a pure, spiritual longing for His presence at all times in our lives. It is love always in an attitude of worship.

> **Listen! My lover is knocking:**
>   **"Open to me, my sister, my darling,**
>   **my dove, my flawless one.**
> **My head is drenched with dew,**
>   **my hair with the dampness of the night."**

> **I have taken off my robe—**
> **must I put it on again?**
> **I have washed my feet—**
> **must I soil them again?**
>
> **Song of Songs 5:2-3**

When the Shunammite woman hears her lover at the door, she is thrown into a quandary about what to do. It reminds me of Peter, when he and the disciples were fishing after Jesus had been resurrected. He had been stripped down, working hard all night, and when he recognized Jesus on the shore *he threw on his robe,* jumped into the water, and swam to meet Him. Sometimes when we finally see the love of our lives we are not quite sure how to come to Him. Do we come as we are or put something on? Are we supposed to cover ourselves or just stand naked before Him?

Peter was so in love with Jesus that he did the opposite of what was practical. He put on his robe and then swam ashore to meet Him! The Shunammite says, "I just took off my robe. Should I put it on again? And what about my feet? Will I get them dirty if I get out of bed? I don't want to meet him with dirty feet!"

We always want to be perfect when we see the Lord, but it seems that King Solomon doesn't give the Shunammite woman a moment more to think about it. She sees his hand come through the latch opening, her passion overwhelms her, and she jumps up to meet him.

My lover thrust his hand through the latch-opening; my heart began to pound for him.

I arose to open for my lover,
    and my hands dripped with myrrh,
    my fingers with flowing myrrh,
    on the handles of the lock.

Song of Songs 5:4-5

He's Gone!

Now begins the Shunammite woman's dark night of the soul.

I opened for my lover,
    but my lover had left; he was gone.
    My heart sank at his departure.

> **I looked for him but did not find him.**
> **I called him but he did not answer.**
>
> **Song of Songs 5:6**

The Shunammite woman is filled with expectancy as she opens her door, only to find that her lover has vanished. She looks everywhere but cannot see him. She calls for him, but he does not answer. This is a picture of a believer entering the dark night of the soul.

Have you ever been in a season of your walk with the Lord where you are faint with love for Him, when your spirit, soul, and body ache for the tangible presence of your Master? This often happens in a season of our lives when we also feel like He might be mistreating us. Our prayers go a little like this. "I don't know if You realize this, Lord, and I'm kind of afraid to say it, but I don't think You are treating me very good right now. I mean, I've given You everything and worked hard for You, and today I'm told my daughter has been raped and the authorities think I did it."

Several years later, just before we experienced the great spiritual breakthrough in Toronto, my prayers went something like this, "Lord, I'm pressing in trying to hear from You and I'm getting nothing. Where are You? What are You doing to me? What is happening here? Do I need to fast more, pray more, do more? Should I change something in my life to be more presentable to You? I'm desperate, Lord. Fill me or kill me!"

That last statement, of course, became the title of our book on how revival and the Father's love came to Linda and me, our family, and our church. At that point in my life when I prayed, "Fill me or kill me," my heart was fainting to have any significant contact with the Lord of my life, and He soon showed up in the most unexpected and wonderful ways! However, for years after Joelle's rape I had been in this dark place where it seemed He was silent.

Flowing Myrrh

Are you in a season when you feel like God may have abandoned you but you are afraid to say it? Have you wondered if He was breaking all His rules about how to treat His children because of the way He seems to be treating you — and then wondered if you originally made up the rules to please yourself or misunderstood His rules in the first place? Are you talking to Him more than ever and hearing less than ever or nothing at all? Have you had a theological argument with yourself over whether or not He could forsake you because His Word says He will never forsake you? If you answered yes to any of these questions, you might be in a dark night of the soul!

In Song of Songs 5:4-5, the Shunammite woman's heart is pounding with anticipation only to be terribly disappointed in verse 6. What was all that about?

There are times when the Lord comes very close to us and we come very close to Him. Then He puts His hand in a new place, we think He's coming even closer, and He seems to disappear on us! But something else has happened. He came with fresh oil, dripping with myrrh, and now it is all over the doorknob. Somehow we know He still loves us and there is a reason for all this. Perhaps the next place He wants to lead us will require our hands to be dripping with myrrh. Maybe He wants us to be always flowing with myrrh.

What is the significance of myrrh? Myrrh appears in Song of Songs earlier, and there it signifies a deep commitment to self-denial, surrender — and suffering for the Lord, if necessary. Myrrh indicates abandoning all selfish and self-centered desires and desiring only the Lord. It says, "I'm all Yours, Lord. I'm not holding back anything from You. I'm not holding on to any personal agendas. I just want Your will for my life. Everything I am and have is Yours, and nothing and no one is more important to me than You."

Myrrh is also used in Exodus 30 when a young man who had been in the family of Levi came to dedicate himself as a priest in the house of the Lord for the rest of his life. They anointed him with myrrh to symbolize his full surrender to the Lord. He dedicated his life to serve God forever.

Myrrh was used in the life of Esther. Before she was called into the presence of the king, every day they would dip her in myrrh. This indicated her complete submission to the king's wishes, and that her sole desire in life was to please him.

I believe our Lord is calling the Church today into a new level of surrender and intimacy, and He wants us to take our beauty treatments! We become more and more beautiful as we put away any desire to please ourselves and increase our desire to please Him. He wants us to be *flowing myrrh,* no longer coming to Him with our selfish plans and self-will but with hearts that are completely His.

CHAPTER 9

Understanding the Dark Night

All believers experience the dark night of the soul in one form or another, and those who have some understanding of it have a better chance of coming out of it with their faith intact. Sad to say, some believers are hit with it and turn to the world or go back into a life of sin instead of pressing into God, His Word, and seeking the counsel of more mature believers. Linda and I stumbled through ours, and it was hard. But now we can help others understand it, and hopefully they can get through it a little easier.

Have you ever felt like God vanished and left you hanging? I sure did when I sat alone and bewildered in that hospital conference room! I don't believe God instigates these times, but I do believe that, if we let Him, He uses them for His purposes. And when we understand His purposes in them, not only can we go through it, but also we become stronger than ever in Him as a result of it.

We have already talked enough about it that you probably have a good idea what it is, but I have four explanations for what is the dark night of the soul.

1. Shift

The dark night of the soul alerts you to the fact that God is shifting you to a new place in Him. If you are experiencing it, then you can be certain He is transitioning you to the next place in Him, where He will use you more powerfully and reveal Himself to you more than ever before. He is raising your level of intimacy and expectation by raising your desire for Him through a trying time in your life. You know He's there because of the Word, which says He is always with you, and the Holy Spirit lives inside you. But you don't sense His manifest presence. In the dark night you learn to trust Him no matter what you experience.

You know what it's like to be close to Him, and He has absolutely ruined you for anything less. You have heard His voice, felt His touch, and enjoyed the warmth of His love and fellowship. You may even have gone into the third heaven with Him, had an angel or two appear to you, and other supernatural experiences. Now all of a sudden He withdraws His manifest presence. You can still lay hands on people and they will receive from Him through you. You may operate in the gifts of the Spirit and see great miracles and transformation in others, but your own experience with God seems more like a wilderness trail than the Promised Land.

God says in Deuteronomy 31:6, "Be strong and courageous. Do not be afraid or terrified because of them, for the LORD your God goes with you; he will never leave you nor forsake you." You know this, and yet you feel like He's gone. So you try to get Him to "come back" by fasting for days, praying for hours on end, hitting every conference in your region, and looking for anything in your life that needs improvement. You literally wear yourself out trying to get the Holy Spirit to give you goose bumps again! Then one day you stop trying to make it happen and just trust Him whether you feel anything or not. There's the shift!

2. This Is a Test…

The dark night of the soul is a God-ordained test. When we step into it, we always try to explain it in order to get it to stop. We think that something this painful is either because we sinned and God has turned His back on us or the devil is attacking us and we need to get rid of demonic activity. So we hit our faces and repent of everything we can think of, then we stand up and scream at every demon we can name.

If those things were a part of why we are in the terrible trouble we are in, dealing with those issues will help. But in a dark night, after repentance and taking authority are over God still remains distant, and this baffles us. What is happening is that God is enlarging our hearts and strengthening our perseverance. He's not angry with us, and the devil isn't making us miserable. We are simply in a time of testing.

God uses the dark night of the soul to test our hearts, so we can see how badly we really want all of Him. The Shunammite woman went through this test because she prayed to become fully mature and completely intimate with King Solomon. She had said,

> **Awake, north wind,**
> > **and come, south wind!**
> **Blow on my garden,**
> > **that its fragrance may spread abroad.**
> **Let my lover come into his garden**
> > **and taste its choice fruits.**
>
> **Song of Songs 4:16**

When you pray for the north winds (representing adversity) and the south winds (representing anointing and blessing) to blow across your garden, for the lover of your soul to come in and taste your fruit (the fruit of the Spirit), you are asking to be purified. And purification requires fire! To attain the maturity and intimacy she desired with Him, the Shunammite woman first had to be tested and tried, refined like gold as by fire.

Let me paraphrase this. She said, "Lord, it feels so good to be close to You and to be totally abandoned to You. That feels so right to me that I want Your north wind to blow across the garden of my heart and purge me of anything that keeps me from being 100 percent Yours. I want this because I want to be able to carry the anointing and blessing the south wind will bring. That is why I'm in this place of total submission to You. When You bless me and anoint me, I don't want my lack of character to sabotage what You want to do in me and through me."

Being tested of the Lord is not a strange thing. God tests everyone's heart. He tested Adam's heart in the Garden of Eden and He tested Jesus' heart in the wilderness. In Luke 4:1-14 the Bible tells us that the Holy Spirit led Jesus into the wilderness to be tested of the devil. And when He came out of the wilderness after the test, the Bible says He came out in the power of the Holy Spirit!

How often have you prayed, "Lord, please take away anything that would hold me back from loving You and serving You with all my heart and with honor. Purify me and cleanse me of anything that would keep me from moving in the power of Your Holy Spirit!" That is your invitation to the Lord to lead you into a dark night of the soul, to send those north winds of adversity to test your heart. Then He can send the south winds of anointing and blessing!

3. Suffering

The phrase, "dark night of the soul," is not a biblical term. It was first found in the writings of St. John of the Cross, who lived in the 16th century. St. John described a time when nothing in our walk with the Lord makes sense. Trouble is all around us. Jesus seems to have gone on vacation from being our Lord, the Holy Spirit has taken a vow of silence, and we would think the Father is mad at us except that we know His Word says in Romans 4:6-8 that He's not.

Many Christians through the ages, most of them Catholics, have used this term to describe their experience of doing everything right biblically and relationally with God, but suddenly everything in their lives goes crazy and God does not respond to their cries for help. He does not do what they want Him to do, or He does not do it in what they believe to be the right timing. Therefore, they are suffering emotionally and many times physically.

Most Protestants, especially today's Charismatics, believe there is no dark night of the soul because Jesus gave us authority over all the power of the enemy, so our lives should be a walk in the park, with no suffering. But the Bible makes it clear that we can have all authority over the enemy and still experience the sufferings of Christ.

Personally, I have found that there are places in the Spirit that I cannot go until my hands are dripping with myrrh. In other words, I have to have experienced or be experiencing the sufferings of Christ — which I don't like very much — in order to set aside my selfish desires and desire only Him and His will for my life.

> Consider it pure joy, my brothers, whenever you face trials of many kinds, because you know that the testing of your faith develops perseverance.

Perseverance must finish its work so that you may be mature and complete, not lacking anything.

James 1:2-4

Suffering is not pleasant, but God uses it to develop perseverance and the character of Christ in us. He knows that if we don't have the faith and patience to believe Him and His Word regardless of what we are feeling and experiencing, then we won't be able to go the distance to fulfill His call on our lives and reach a place of full contentment in Him that is not based on feelings or circumstances.

4. Silence

When we are born again the Holy Spirit comes to live in us. We cannot live godly lives and obey the Word without Him. When the Holy Spirit breaks through our busy minds to lead us, as He did to me when I began praying in tongues in the emergency room of the hospital, He brings strength and wisdom to keep us moving forward. But in the dark night of the soul we are desperate to hear from Him and He is generally silent. This is how I felt for years after Joelle's rape. We were silent about it, and God seemed to be silent in me.

I would look around me in church and see other believers' faces and know He was talking to them. They were hearing from Him, so He was talking to everyone but me. I got more hungry, more obedient, put myself through fasts and long times of prayer and study — but He was still silent.

I felt like the Shunammite woman in Song of Songs 4:6 (my paraphrase), "I opened for my lover. I opened *wide my whole heart* for Him, but He wasn't there. He left me in silence, and my heart ached."

The worst part of the dark night of the soul is learning to deal with the fact that for some reason the Holy Spirit is not speaking to us like He used to. We must believe He is still there inside us, but for now He is silent. What He is doing is bringing us to a higher level of love, trust, and contentment.

CHAPTER 10

God's Purposes in the Dark Night

Why does God allow the dark night of the soul? We have touched on these purposes in the last couple of chapters, but let's take a more thorough look at what God does in us when we find ourselves in the dark night of the soul.

1. Greater Intimacy and Deeper Connectedness with God

The Scriptures talk often of how suffering is the vehicle God uses to bring us to new levels of intimacy and a deeper connectedness with Him. When the Shunammite rose to open the door for her lover, her hands dripping with myrrh, her heart was wide open to the king. As the bride of Christ, that is how we need to be in order to increase our intimacy with Jesus. We rest in His love and blessing, and He says, "Hey, do you want more of Me?"

We say, "Yes! Yes!" And our hearts begin to pound with expectation. We are waking up to a new level, He rings the doorbell — and runs.

The idea is: He wants us to follow Him! He wants us to catch Him. And He wants us to catch Him flowing with myrrh, fully committed and anointed to love Him in difficult times as well as prosperous times. Are we committed and anointed to love Him and serve Him when we don't know what is happening or what is coming, when we are in that transition place where everything hurts? If we are, we will be ushered into a bright, new place where our intimacy with and connection to Jesus are unfathomable. One of God's purposes in taking us through the dark night of the soul is to simply get close to us, to become even more united with us in the Spirit.

2. Increased Love for God

God sometimes hides from those who already love Him deeply, who love Him with everything they've got. He knows that the desire of their hearts is to love Him even more, so He says, "Oh, I can fix that. I can help you love Me even more."

Then He leads them through a dark night of the soul, where they learn to love Him even when He seems to have vanished. They learn that the deepest love is not based on feelings, goose bumps, and extraordinary supernatural experiences. The deepest love is a choice made in the direst of circumstances, the decision to love when there is no tangible, visible motivation to love.

This is for lovers of God, for those who realize that He is the only One who will ever satisfy their deepest needs and desires. The only dissatisfaction they have is with themselves and their capacity to love Him and serve Him. They pray, "Lord, I recognize at times there are distractions that come into my life. I recognize there are things that still catch my attention and take my eyes off of You, and I don't want anything to distract me from You! I don't want to love or desire anything more than You. Lord, You know that I just want to love You." He answers by playing hide and seek!

When my daughters were little, I would come home from work and yell, "Daddy's home!" They would run to meet me and jump into my arms, then I would whirl them around in midair and we would kiss each other all over. But sometimes, if I wanted to heighten their anticipation, I would yell, "Daddy's home!" and then run and hide or play "catch-me-if-you-can." They would run towards me and I would open my arms like I was going to catch them, but at the last minute I would dodge them and make them chase me.

Whether I hid or ran, my objective was to be caught! I wanted them to show me how much they wanted me and needed me. I would encourage them to run faster and try harder, "Come on. Give it another shot. Come on, you can catch me!" If I was hiding, I'd make little sounds to give them an idea of where I was. All because I wanted them to find me, grab hold of me, and hug and kiss me. I wanted to be their sole passion at that moment. All their toys, their concerns, their homework, and their chores were forgotten because the most important thing was chasing Dad!

When we cry for God to help us to love Him more, I believe He sticks His hand through the lattice, rattles the doorknob to wake us up, and when we come running to Him, expecting and completely focused on Him, He runs because He wants us to chase Him. He wants us to find Him. And something happens as we chase Him. In the difficulty and trial of running in the darkness around us, our capacity and understanding of what it means to love God more than anyone or anything else in life grows stronger and deeper.

3. Loving and Willing Obedience to God

God is longing for a people who will stand in absolute obedience and love with Him. No matter what happens in their life, in their environment, in their church, in their marriage, with their children, or with their nation's government and economy, He desires His sons and daughters to cheerfully and quickly obey Him. We are Jesus' bride, and the bride of Christ ought to obey her Bridegroom without question, knowing that He only has her best interest at heart because He loves her with an everlasting love.

If we are to become the bride worthy of Jesus, we must submit to His sufferings. We must pick up our cross and follow Him in dying to ourselves and living only for Him. We may or may not suffer the exact same things He did, but we will learn His sufferings. He experienced rejection, ridicule, beatings, whipping, a crown of thorns, being nailed to the cross, and just before His death feeling forsaken by God. That sounds like a dark night of the soul to me!

If God is going to give Jesus a bride to match Him in love and obedience, we are probably going to go through a season or maybe more than one season of the dark night of the soul to become that perfect match. This doesn't frighten me because I have been through it and have seen the fruit of it. Today I am more sensitive to His voice and more quick to obey the Holy Spirit and the Word of God than I was before I went through the dark night because my love and reverence for Him are greater.

When I was being accused of raping my daughter, I would have done anything the Lord asked me to do to end that tormenting situation. When the situation was resolved and we took our girls home, you would think I would have been happy as a clam; but the dark night continued because God's purposes were greater than just easing my discomfort. He wanted me to do anything He asked me to do simply because I loved Him and not just to get out of a bad situation. He wanted my desire to be His pleasure and not my own. And He was doing this for me, because ultimately the only thing that was going to make me happy was loving Him as He loved me — without any strings attached.

4. Pure Heart Toward God

The dark night of the soul is part of God's sovereign training program, which causes our hearts to mature and to be purified. In the silence, we call to Him and He doesn't answer. This is a shock because we are used to Him answering us. When we do all the things we do and go to all the places we can think to go to try to hear from Him and He still doesn't say anything, a light finally goes on inside us that says, "God is going to have His way in this, so I might as well just relax and trust Him."

Then we come face-to-face with what our motives are in seeking Him in the first place. Do we have a "works" mentality? Are we still trying to control as much as possible — even trying to make God speak to us when we want Him to speak?

It's amazing how strongholds in our lives emerge when we walk through a dark time and a little light of truth we never would have considered before begins to shine through. Sometimes, in order to break down all those rigid, legalistic rules and religious limitations we have placed on God and ourselves through the years, He will take us through a time when none of our religious formulas and rituals work. He cannot be found in any of them. This brings us to a place of humility where we can allow the Holy Spirit to free us of all the religious foolishness and just cry, "You're God! You're God! You're God! All I want is You!"

In the dark night we throw open our hearts and minds to receive a bigger picture and a purer perspective. If we submit to and continue to run after God instead of rebelling and running from Him during the dark night of the soul, He will purify our hearts and make us even greater vessels of honor. We will come through it all and find ourselves no longer bound by narrow minds and impure motives.

CHAPTER 11

How Other Believers May Respond

Unless they have gone through the dark night of the soul themselves and have also allowed God to do what He wanted to do in them, other believers probably will not understand what you are going through. There are two common responses that you can expect from many Christian friends and family when you cooperate with God in your dark night of the soul: persecution and rejection. This is especially true for those who are entrenched in the extremes of the message of faith, prosperity, and healing.

Notice I said "the extremes." There is a sound and true biblical message of faith, prosperity, and healing. But some have taken it and run into a ditch with it, becoming legalistic and mean-spirited. You have probably met some of them. If your loved one died instead of being healed, they told you that they died because they either didn't have enough faith or they must have been in sin. These are the people who look down their noses at you when you are struggling financially but consider you a tower of faith if you live in a big house and drive an expensive car. In a nutshell, they live by formulas of faith and outward appearances and have forgotten that faith works by love.

When these people see you in the middle of a catastrophic mess, and all you can say is that you don't know what's going on, but you know He is working something in you — you are messing them up! Their formulas say that you are supposed to have victory, to be on top, to be the head and not the tail. Christians aren't supposed to be broken and clinging to Jesus for dear life — and you not only offend them, but the thought that you might be going through a genuine biblical experience of suffering just scares them!

If these believers will get honest about their fear, they will go to the Word and the Spirit for further instruction. But if they refuse to admit their fear, they will continue to hold to their formulas and reject and persecute you as a means of coping. When that happens, you should just forgive them and pray for them.

The Misdirected Watchmen

The watchmen found me
>**as they made their rounds in the city.**
>**They beat me, they bruised me;**
>**they took away my cloak,**
>**those watchmen of the walls!**

>>**Song of Songs 5:7**

There are good watchmen and misdirected watchmen. The misdirected watchmen consider themselves "professional watchmen," experts in the body of Christ who know just enough of the Word of God to believe they know it all. They have grown into a level of spiritual maturity. They have experienced walking in the Spirit and have prayed in the authority of Jesus' name. They see themselves as mature believers, as solid citizens in the kingdom of God. Some of them are in the ministry, teaching and preaching. Some are ministers in the marketplace. Some are homemakers. They watch, believing that they know how the things of God are supposed to work in the life of a believer.

One day they watch you and see that you are not behaving and talking like they believe you should. They might rebuke you. They might talk about you behind your back. And if they are your pastor they might even make a public example of you, talking about you from the pulpit — without mentioning your name, of course.

What has just happened to these mature believers is that they have taken their eyes off Jesus and put them on you. A good watchman is watching for the Lord, for the move of the Spirit, for the Father's will. Misdirected watchmen are watching other people. They are not walking in the Spirit. They are not aware of how God is moving. Even though they love Him, they have missed the direction He is taking in your life and possibly in their life and the body of Christ because their eyes are on you. You are not fitting their mold and pattern of

Christianity, and instead of questioning the Lord and opening up to Him for fresh revelation and greater intimacy, they persecute and reject you.

Dealing with the Misdirected Watchmen

When you go through the dark night of the soul, your life does not fit the misdirected watchmen's theology, experience, and especially their spiritual comfort zone. Basically, you just rub them the wrong way. Instead of going to God and dealing with their offense, they focus on you and how you are offending them.

The main thing that offends them is your love walk with the Lord. They are irritated by your extravagant love relationship with Him, believing you are too subjective and emotional. For that reason they don't really approve of burning hearts. They will say, "No wonder you are going through such a bad time. You're too emotional!" and try to bring you back under their religious pattern.

These religious watchmen have become carnal and jealous without realizing it. They make their rounds in the city, and when they find a believer or another ministry whose hearts are passionate for more of the presence and power of God, they beat them (take cheap shots), bruise them (deeply wound them), and take away their cloaks (denounce their manner of worship, their theology, and their ministry).

Some churches experience revival and enter a dark night of the soul simply because of the carnality and jealousy of other churches in their city. However, God uses this to refine their love for Him and set them free from strongholds of sin and religious attitudes.

When God takes you into the dark night of the soul, the greatest test will be surviving the attitudes and words of mature believers who do not understand what God is doing with you. Don't be distracted by them! Keep your eyes on Jesus and let your confession be exactly what the bride of Christ's confession has always been, "Although I can't explain everything that is happening to me and I don't have full revelation about it yet, His banner over me is love." Then God can move in *your* life!

There are times when watchmen who have been entrusted with leadership and authority may become so threatened by a burning heart or so embarrassed by the troubles they are going through that they will actually remove them from ministry. "They took away my cloak" (Song of Songs 5:7). This is not always an attack of the enemy! In a dark night of the soul, God may allow our ministry to be set aside for a while, especially if we have had a tendency to wrap our hearts around ministry more than Him. He does not want us to be rooted and grounded in the love of our ministry instead of the love of Christ. We can literally get addicted to the "high" we get from the anointing when we are ministering and worshipping instead of keeping our hearts pure.

The dark night of the soul requires us to deal with misdirected watchmen in love and with forgiveness, while we recognize God's purposes in the trials we are going through. He wants to set US free! When we walk in love and forgiveness and submit to Him in everything, He can continue to work in them and in us. Just like Jesus, who hung on the cross and forgave people for not knowing what they were doing to Him, we can forgive those who persecute us and reject us in our darkest hours. And when we do that, we will have dealt with the misdirected watchmen in a way that will bring honor to the Lord and maturity and freedom into our own lives.

The Gift of Persecution

As the bride of Christ, we will be persecuted just as He was when He was on the earth because we are also His body, carrying out His will here on earth. Jesus gave us a lot of wisdom about persecution and how to handle it. Just imagine He is sitting with you right now, talking to you, as you read His words.

> "Blessed are you when people insult you, persecute you and falsely say all kinds of evil against you because of me. Rejoice and be glad, because great is your reward in heaven, for in the same

way they persecuted the prophets who were before you."

Matthew 5:11-12

Jesus is saying, "You must have the right attitude and perspective about persecution. It is a gift! You should rejoice because you are going to be greatly rewarded by God. So when they talk about you behind your back, insult you and your relationship with Me by calling your burning heart 'overemotional,' and even take away your ministry for a while, just smile and continue following Me. Love them in spite of how they treat you, just like I did on the cross. Then one day, just like Me, you will come out of that dark night in the resurrection power of the Holy Spirit!"

In the hospital, the detective threw me against the wall and said in a demonic voice, "You listen to me, preacher! You have no say in this matter!" He called me "preacher." And the tone of his voice let me understand that he was under the influence of a demon that hated me and hated Jesus. At that moment I made the choice to continue speaking what I believed was true, but to do it with love and respect. This was one of those points in time when God enlarged my heart because I chose to be like Jesus.

> "You have heard that it was said, 'Love your neighbor and hate your enemy.' But I tell you: Love your enemies and pray for those who persecute you, that you may be sons of your Father in heaven. He causes his sun to rise on the evil and the good, and sends rain on the righteous and the unrighteous. If you love those who love you, what reward will you get? Are not even the tax collectors doing that? And if you greet only your brothers, what are you doing more than others? Do not even pagans do that? Be perfect, therefore, as your heavenly Father is perfect."
>
> Matthew 5:43-48

Persecution is a gift that enables us to walk in love and have a perfect heart like our Father in heaven. When you are going through persecution, it doesn't feel very good. I didn't like the way that detective was treating me. But those sufferings took me deeper into the meaning of knowing the love of Christ. My ability to

How Other Believers May Respond

love my enemies expanded because it had to! The only alternative was to become bitter and tormented, which would have done no one any good. My heart was enlarged because it had to enlarge in order to persevere in faith.

When you emerge from this time, with a greater capacity to love and be loved, you are dripping with the oil of God's anointing in the same way Jesus came out of the wilderness in the power of the Holy Spirit. You will be able to minister in power and compassion just as He did because you are no longer bound by a lack of compassion for your enemies or little understanding of the purposes of God in suffering for Jesus.

CHAPTER 12

What Does God Want?

What response is God looking for from us in the dark night of the soul? I believe there are three things He is looking to produce in us. After going through it several times in my own life, I won't say that these three things will shorten the time in the dark night, but I do know that they will make it easier to submit to God in that trying time.

Humility

O daughters of Jerusalem, I charge you —
    if you find my lover,
    what will you tell him?
    Tell him I am faint with love.

Song of Songs 5:8

The first thing God desires to see in you as a result of the dark night of the soul is humility. In this passage of Scripture, the Shunammite has just been beat up, bruised, and robbed of her cloak by the watchmen who are supposed to be her friends and protectors. Most of us would say, "When you see my love, would you tell Him something for me? I'm not very happy with Him. In fact, I'm really ticked off. I don't understand why He's jerking me around like this, and I'm hurt, offended, and angry."

But the Shunammite woman says something entirely different. She says, "Look, I'm not understanding things very well right now, so if you happen to see my lover, would you tell him that I am fainting with love for him and would like to see him as soon as possible?"

This teaches us what to say when all hell breaks loose in our lives and Jesus seems to have disappeared. "Lord, I'm not hearing from You, and I don't know where You are or what You are doing, but I love You more than ever. I need You more than ever. And if You are listening to me, please come to me. Help me to understand, and tell me what You want me to do. I'm all beat up and bruised, and people are talking badly about me, but I forgive them and all I care about is You. I just want You."

I believe the Lord is pleased when He hears these words because now He can share great revelation with us. We are humble and teachable, and our hearts and minds are open to hear anything He has to say. When Linda sat in the bathroom of that cockroach-infested hotel room in Phoenix, totally broken, she received a word from the Lord that completely unraveled the enemy's schemes and set our family free. Because of her humility, God could speak to her and use her.

We didn't recognize it at the time, but now we understand that we must maintain that attitude of humility at all times. We learned that from going through the dark night of the soul in the years that followed Joelle's rape. Humility is one of the things the Lord wants to bring forth in our lives so that He can reveal Himself and entrust us with more and more in His kingdom.

Tenderness of Heart

O daughters of Jerusalem, I charge you.

Song of Songs 5:8

The Shunammite woman has been beat up, bruised, and insulted by the watchmen who claim to be mature believers, and instead of being offended and reacting in pride she becomes childlike. In her brokenness, instead of being unforgiving and becoming bitter she chooses to forgive and have faith as a little child. This makes her heart genuinely tender toward the Lord — and toward His body.

Notice that she no longer addresses the watchmen, but she tells the "daughters of Jerusalem" that if they see her lover, would they please tell him that she is faint with love for him. This gives us great insight into what our attitude toward the body of Christ should be when some members reject us and persecute us. Although one part of the body rejected and persecuted her, the Shunammite woman is so tender and childlike that she still has faith in the body of Christ. She doesn't stop fellowship in the church just because she was treated badly by a few believers. She turns to the daughters of Jerusalem for help.

As pastors we have seen many believers through the years who get hurt and offended in one church and stop going to church altogether. Then there are those who are involved in a great move of the Spirit and run into some believers who aren't, and they are rejected by them. As a result, the believers in the renewal movement turn around and reject and look down their noses at anyone who is not involved in the latest move of the Spirit.

I run into believers all the time who have been beat up by other Christians, and so they reject all Christians. Or they've been beat up by people who aren't in the "river," so they reject everybody who's not in the river. Every time they do this they lose pieces of their hearts. They grow just a bit colder and less tender toward the Lord and toward His people.

Genuine tenderness that comes forth from a heart that has been beaten, bruised, and broken is precious to the Lord. It shows that you have chosen to follow in His footsteps. In the face of the greatest motivations not to love, you have chosen the walk of love instead of becoming arrogant and offended. In essence, you have chosen to be like Jesus, to take up your cross and follow Him in love and forgiveness.

Steadfast Love

Tell him I am faint with love.

Song of Songs 5:8

After tremendous trial and persecution, the Shunammite woman is still absolutely lovesick for King Solomon, revealing her steadfast love for him. Instead of becoming offended, withdrawing and rebelling, or running away to find another man to love, she continues loving and pursuing him.

As believers, we need to stop being offended every time things don't go the way we want or expect them to go. We should never stop praying and seeking the Lord when He doesn't do what we want or expect Him to do. We can run from church to church, trying to find some believers who will treat us the way we want to be treated; we can refuse to darken a church door again because of how a few Christians treated us; or we can reject and gossip about those in the body who reject us; but none of these alternatives is going to make us happy or help us to grow.

Nothing will make us happy or enable us to grow except the love of God. Being with Him and walking in His love are the only things that will satisfy us.

I have noticed that in renewal churches believers get so deeply touched by the Holy Spirit and have such wonderful, powerful encounters with God that they can easily slip into the assumption that says, "I'm so close to God now. I have such favor now, and I'm so much more mature now. This new place I have found in Him should keep me from hard times or at least it should keep me *in* the hard times."

Then they enter the dark night of the soul, and God says to them, "Will you love Me with your whole heart, hard times or not? I am not a quick fix for you. Will you continue running after Me? Will you have faith in My love whether you feel the goose bumps or not? Or are you going to get bitter and decide all this renewal stuff is just another fad for disillusioned believers, when your life suddenly becomes difficult and even painful?"

God wants you to be steadfast and unshakeable in the knowledge of His love for you and your love for Him — no matter what happens or how you are treated by other people, including the body of Christ. He wants to know that your love for Him is pure, based on His pure love for you.

Do you love the Lord so you can be comfortable and have pleasure?

Do you love the Lord so you can have extraordinary, supernatural experiences?

Do you love the Lord so you can have His power and authority to heal the sick and cast out demons?

Do you love the Lord for any reason other than just because He is your loving Lord and Savior and King?

Like anyone else, Jesus wants us to love Him for Him — not because of what He does but because of who He is. He wants to know that no matter what we go through, in good times and bad times, we love Him more and more. Our hearts are always faint with love for Him. We never get enough of His presence and His Word. Our greatest joy is communing with Him, whether it's just sitting in His presence or receiving great revelation.

When we are faint with love for Him, we will do anything He asks of us joyfully. We know that nothing is impossible with Him, so we trust Him completely. That's why, if we fully submit to Him and continue loving and pursuing Him through the dark night of the soul, our faith will never fail. We can continue to serve Him with honor and power and glory and blessing even in our darkest hours.

God Performs His Word

There is one more thing that God brings forth while we are going through and especially after we have been through a dark night of the soul: reaching out to others to help them in their dark night. Now Linda and I, our girls, and our church family have a testimony to share that is based on the rock-solid conviction that God will perform His Word in our lives. Everything that He originally spoke to us years ago has come to pass, and we want the world to know about it!

We realize that when Joelle was raped it was an all-out attack of the enemy on our family. A loving heavenly Father does not orchestrate the rape of His children! This was a diabolical plot of the devil's to destroy our family, and there were times over the years that followed, in our dark night of the soul, when he almost succeeded. But we remembered the word of the Lord that He gave us through one of His prophets just before all this happened. She had said, "This church is going to become very powerful. I see the Lord using your family as a sacrifice poured out over the church. It's going to create a brokenness in you that is going to lead to the healing of many. The church is going to be very strong and very powerful, but your family is going to be used as a sacrifice for that to happen."

God knew what the enemy had planned for us. He also knew we were not in a place spiritually to prevent it from happening. As Linda said, we didn't know that we should pray and ask God about a word of prophecy, especially one that gave us a warning of things to come. God knew we would just keep going to Disneyland no matter what, and that tragedy would strike us. But God wasn't going to let Satan have the last word!

In Romans 8:28, it says that God works all things together for our good because we love Him and are called according to His purposes. That is really what our story is all about. He took our dark night of the soul and the terrible events of that Christmas vacation and used it for our good. He brought our family through the fire, refining us and purifying our hearts. As a result, today we are more in love with Him and each other than we could ever have imagined before all this happened. We are *No Longer Bound* by the traumas of our past.

What's more astonishing is that the miracle right in the middle of all of it was Joelle herself. God supernaturally spared her all the anguish and difficulties most people go through when they have been molested as children. In our darkest hours, God set her in our midst — growing up unscathed and untouched by the enemy's vicious attack upon her as a child — to remind us that He was not only still in charge but also still loved us and cared about us deeply.

CHAPTER 13

Getting Delivered

"Come, let us return to the LORD.
He has torn us to pieces
> but he will heal us;
>
> he has injured us
>
> but he will bind up our wounds.

After two days he will revive us;
> on the third day he will restore us,
>
> that we may live in his presence.

Let us acknowledge the LORD;
> let us press on to acknowledge him.
>
> As surely as the sun rises,
>
> he will appear;
>
> he will come to us like the winter rains,
>
> like the spring rains that water the earth."

Hosea 6:1-3

Joel: When the enemy came in like a flood, the Lord raised up a standard against him and his plans of destruction for our family. First, He used the attack on Joelle to get us to wake up and see that we had a real and very evil enemy. Next, He caused me to be supernaturally proven innocent and to be released from the authorities in Phoenix. Then He gave us a Christian counselor, who spent a year with us, teaching us how to communicate our thoughts and feelings and how to take care of issues in a constructive way. But overall, He created a tremendous hunger and thirst for more of the Holy Spirit within our hearts.

In time the Holy Spirit led us to people and places He used to impart more of the presence and power of the Holy Spirit. We experienced waves of the Father's love washing over our hearts and minds. We had many experiences of soaking in His power and love. We had powerful encounters with Him where He poured into us and the pain left us. (You can read about these wonderful encounters in *Fill Me or Kill Me*.) We were being loved by God like we had never been loved before. And with these encounters came a stronger and more authoritative ministry anointing in the areas of prophecy, healing, deliverance, dreams, and visions.

What happened next was a tremendous breakthrough for us, and we believe it can be a great breakthrough for you as well. When we were on a ministry trip to Russia and the Ukraine, we had breakfast with John Arnott. He knew our story and how God was healing us, touching us, and renewing us. He told us how wounded he had been in his life, and then explained how God had delivered him and his wife Carol from their wounds of the past.

We said to him, "John, you are one of the most genuinely loving persons we have ever met. How did you get to this place?" What John said launched us into the joy of getting delivered.

John said, "I'm going to tell you something I tell all my friends and all my leaders, but very few of them do it. Anyone who wants to carry the love, perseverance, and anointing of God for the long haul absolutely must go see one of the Restoring The Foundations ministry teams. This ministry was founded by Chester and Betsy

Kylstra.[1] I want to challenge you to do what Carol and I have done — go through a healing week with their ministry. We do it every year just to keep current with all forgiveness issues."

He explained their ministry to us. We didn't understand how it all worked, but we said we would do it because we trusted him. He said there was a several-months waiting list for many of the teams, even longer for Chester and Betsy Kylstra, because they were busy training teams to help more people receive healing. However, he would call them and see if they would put us on the list. We didn't know it at the time, but we were about to be launched to a level of healing and cleansing we could not even imagine.

It Begins

Linda: We ended up waiting for two years before we were able to meet with the Kylstras. However, the time finally came and we went for ministry, having no idea

---

[1] www.RestoringTheFoundations.org

what we were getting into. But we knew God had connected us to John and Carol Arnott, and when He connects you with people and they tell you that you ought to do something, then the Holy Spirit probably wants you to do it!

Two weeks before we left, I had dreams about foundations. I dreamed that old house foundations and building foundations were being ripped up and new ones were being laid in their place. I told Joel, "God is about to give me new foundations." But I didn't know what that meant. When we got to the Kylstras in North Carolina, I found out the name of their ministry is "Restoring the Foundations" ("RTF")!

We were there for seven days of personal, in-depth deliverance ministry. On Sunday evening Chester and Betsy Kylstra sat with us and said, "Tell us everything that is bothering you."

Immediately we gave each other a look that meant — "Oh no!" We were happy, and who wants to drag up old stuff? But they wouldn't let us get away with that, so we just started talking. All they did was take notes and ask questions. They just kept digging for information in every part of our lives and writing.

I wondered, *What in the world are they writing down?*

After three hours of this they told us we could go to bed. They said they wanted to see me privately in the morning for three hours. Then they wanted to meet with Joel privately for three hours. We would do this all week until Saturday, when they would bring us back together.

We would also have about three hours of homework to do each day. And they said we had to make a commitment not to discuss any of our issues with each other. When we saw each other we were just to relax.

My session came Monday morning, and I have to tell you I was about as nervous as a fish out of water. They continued their interview with me and just kept taking notes. They told me they were looking for all the sins of the fathers and resulting curses in my life.

The sins of the fathers represent the accumulation of all sins committed by our ancestors. It is the heart tendency (iniquity) that we inherit from our forefathers to rebel against or to be disobedient to God's laws and commandments. It is the inherited propensity to sin, particularly in ways that represent perversion and twisted character. The accumulation continues through the generations until God's conditions for repentance are met.

In other words, they were looking at every ancestral door of iniquity that was ever opened on both sides of our family lines. By uncovering issues where the demonic was empowered in our lives, we could get free in those areas.

In that week I found out that just about every door that could be opened to the devil had been opened on both sides of my family! If you have gone through any type of deliverance ministry, you know what I am talking about. It was a little overwhelming, especially since Joel and I had been through all sorts of deliverance ministry before we came to RTF.

Ungodly Beliefs

On Tuesday the Kylstras read all of the ungodly beliefs that had come out of my mouth in both of my interviews. An ungodly belief does not line up with the Word of God. An example would be saying, "I have always had an anger problem, and I have done all I know to get free, so I guess I always will have this problem."

That statement is an ungodly belief because it is not what the Bible says about the born-again believer. John 8:36 says that whoever the Son sets free is free! There is no "except…" or "unless…" in the verse.

After listening to all of the ungodly beliefs I had said, Chester and Betsy worked with me to replace them with godly beliefs. My job was to find Scripture to prove every ungodly belief was a lie. This was a big assignment but a valuable one.

Take anger, for instance. Ephesians 4:26 NKJV says, "Be angry, and do not sin." If you have a terrible anger problem, chances are you have prayed about it, received counseling about it, and maybe even taken an anger management course. But it doesn't seem like any of this has helped. You are still prone to go out of control when something upsets you.

At this point you usually throw up your hands and say, "I guess I will just always have this anger problem. I know God's not the problem. My problem is too deep. I'm just not a very nice person."

Those are ungodly beliefs. But my next question was, "I still don't know how to change my behavior or my thought process. So what do I do?"

Inner Healing

After I had written all my godly beliefs with their corresponding scriptures I was ready to go through inner healing. This was on Thursday, our fourth day. The Kylstras explained that this would deal with soul/spirit hurts.

Soul/spirit hurts are on the inside of a person. They are wounds to the soul or the spirit that are carried and experienced within. They are not physical, and they cannot be seen. Their presence is revealed by their symptoms, which are manifested evidence of unhealed emotions, behaviors, and thoughts.

They said, "We want you to close your eyes and sit quietly. We are going to ask the Lord to take you back to any memory or picture that He wants to show you. We want Him to show you what caused you to empower the strongholds in your life and open doors to demonic influence. What is a memory or picture that caused you great pain?"

I immediately opened my eyes and said, "Oh, this doesn't work for me. I tried this with one of our pastors, and I didn't ever see anything."

They said, "Well, we think you will this time because we have taken you through a process of getting rid of wrong thoughts — ungodly beliefs. So, are you willing to try it?"

I said, "Of course," and closed my eyes. I prayed, "Father, show me what empowered all of my pain from the past. Show me what empowered the demonic."

I immediately had a picture. I had never seen anything like it. Then I had a memory. I had had this memory many times, but I never understood that it caused the pain that had built a stronghold of lies in my mind.

My mother had wanted me to learn a poem and recite it for all the ladies at our little country church. I was so excited! I learned it perfectly, so that I could just rattle it off. But when I stood up to speak in front of all those women, I froze with fear. It was so quiet. Everyone was looking at me. They waited and waited. And I just stood there. I couldn't speak.

I heard them urge me to speak. I saw the disgusted looks on some of their faces. I heard my mother prompt me and try to get me started. But inside I said, "No, never again." That day I made a vow deep inside me. "I will never say anything. They can't make me, and I won't. I will never talk to a stranger again."

The Kylstras asked me to take a second look. They said, "Do you see anything else?"

I saw myself as a tiny, little girl, ashamed and embarrassed.

They told me this was the point where a demon of fear, control, and shame had entered my life. It was the place where demonic empowerment had taken place. I went through prayers of forgiveness and release of all involved in that situation. And I forgave myself for not performing.

Then they asked me, "Where was Jesus in the situation?" And this time I saw Him in the audience, cheering me on! I was able not only to say the poem but also to sing, to dance, and to be cute as a bug for the ladies. All of a sudden I was an adult preaching, and the Lord took a sock out of my mouth. I remembered a prophetic word that I had been given in 2000. "God is going to take the sock out of your mouth, and you are going to be able to teach and preach to the people."

D Day

Thursday was a tremendous day, but Chester and Betsy had told me all week that Friday was going to be "D Day," the day of deliverance. We were not going to attempt to cast any demons out until Friday. So on Thursday after the inner healing session, they said,

"You might be uncomfortable tonight, but we have bound it all up, so you should be okay."

I said, "Awesome."

They had assured me that all the days of ministry we had gone through during the week led up to the day of deliverance. By that time, having dismantled the lies and ungodly beliefs and having discovered how they gained a stronghold, anything demonic would easily come out.

Now you need to understand something about my personality. I had a feeling something major was going to happen. These people were deep, and they seemed to know what they were doing. So I had called home all week long to tell my kids, "Get ready. I am going to go through deliverance on Friday, and I hope I manifest." In case you don't know what "manifest" means, it is when a demon comes out or off (assignment cancelled) and you know it because something dramatic happens.

I wanted it all. I wanted to go to a new level of freedom. I also wanted to be sure that if there was a demon that had attached itself to me, I would know when it left. I was in good hands. I knew that the Kylstras could handle whatever happened.

"D Day" finally came. We prayed through all sorts of categories of common strongholds and their various manifestations. Sure enough, when we got to one of them I felt myself go off into a "trancelike state" that was not the Holy Spirit. I had never experienced anything like it. I was caught in a trance, and I couldn't get out of it. Then I was unable to talk. I felt like I was stuck.

Chester and Betsy were right on top of it, immediately taking authority over the demon and setting me free. It happened about five times, and then it was gone. Although I couldn't pull myself out of this frozen trancelike condition on my own, it wasn't scary in the least. It was very peaceful. And after they got that "strongman" off of me I felt a freedom I have never had in my entire life.

On the way home in the Atlanta airport, in the midst of hundreds of people, I had a tremendous experience. Carrying my purse and pulling my carry-on, suddenly

I felt as if I was "going up." It felt as if I was leaving my body.

I was so surprised at what I was feeling that my first thought was negative, that perhaps the demonic was manifesting again. I grabbed Joel and began to dig my fingers into his arm. He saw what was happening and threw our bags down.

Joel looked at me and said, "I see an open heaven over you. I see an open portal, full of clean light, going up and down into the heavens." He kept saying, "It's clean and open! I can see it! Wow! It's like an open channel, and it's clean, like for the first time in generations!"

Right in front of everyone he bound any demonic interference and blessed me to go into the high places with the Lord. We realized that where the demonic had previously blocked me, I was now free to soar with the Lord and perhaps even begin to travel in the Spirit as Philip and John and Paul had done in the Bible.

Deliverance Is a Lifelong Process

You might be thinking, *Isn't this a little personal? Why are you sharing all of this?*

Nothing is too personal when it comes to the saving, healing, delivering power of Jesus Christ that transforms a life. It should all be told. My testimony is something God can use to set you free, and then your testimony can set someone else free. And we are all in a continual process of getting delivered. There is always more!

There is always more freedom.

There is always another level of victory.

There is always more of the Father's love.

There is always more of the Father's heart.

I tell you my story, and that lets you know that if I can do this, you can as well.

Joel:

Because of the great healing and deliverance we experienced, we now have the same weeklong course at our church conducted by the staff of RTF. It is called "A Healing Week." Many of our congregation members have gone through this course and have had a fantastic experience. Because of God's grace Linda and I are always going deeper in the Lord, and we want those we lead to go deeper with us. (You can read all about this course in For Further Help, which is just after Chapter 14, and we encourage you to apply.)

From time to time throughout our lives, the Lord will want to do something new in our hearts. The Holy Spirit will show us a place in our soul or spirit where we have become caught in generational patterns of iniquity. Why does He do this? So He can set us free!

We have no reason to be afraid when He is leading us in deliverance. Every time He invites us to come out of shame, fear, control, or some other pattern of iniquity, we should be excited! More freedom awaits us. More victory is set before us. And the freer we become, the more He can use us to set others free.

Most important, the more we empty ourselves of the baggage from the past, the more Jesus can fill us with Himself, the more we can know the Father's love, and the more we can walk in the power of the Holy Spirit. This is really why Linda and I welcome those times of getting delivered!

CHAPTER 14

Where We Are Today

Today we are *No Longer Bound* by our childhood fears and dysfunctions because God brought us through a dark night of the soul that exposed those strongholds, tore down the structure of lies in our minds, and gave us the ability to trust Him with our lives completely. We are *No Longer Bound* because we submitted to His purposes, continued to love and pursue Him and His Word, and allowed Him to refine us, heal us, deliver us, and renew our minds.

That last statement sounds like it was all up to us, but we know that it was all Him! He loved us, He brought us through those north winds of adversity, He brought the south winds of anointing and blessing, and He delivered us. Today, the word of the Lord that the prophetess delivered years ago is coming to pass. Our church is experiencing great renewal and revival, and our family's testimony of the Father's love is opening hearts from all walks of life to the Lord and His healing, delivering power so that they are *No Longer Bound*.

All for You

God wants you to be free. That's why the Lord gave Linda the word "Shanakey!" He wanted us to tell our story so He could use it to heal your heart from old wounds that have been holding you back and keeping you down.

Are you bound by a trauma from your past that has caused you to walk in a dark night of the soul? Maybe you were sexually molested and now you are dealing with homosexuality, lesbianism, pedophilia, pornography, or sexual addiction. Maybe you cut yourself and hurt yourself because of shame and guilt over your past.

Perhaps you suffer from anorexia and bulimia and really hate yourself at times. Have you experienced moments when you wondered whether you wouldn't be better off dead because you feel trapped in a lifestyle, compulsion, or addiction that is slowly destroying you?

Perhaps you have asked Jesus into your heart, but you still have areas of your life where, instead of experiencing victory and freedom, you still feel bound.

You don't have to live like this anymore!

God wants you to be free of the trauma of your past and get you through this dark night of the soul so that you are healed and strong in Him, so that you can live the abundant life Jesus died to give you. We encourage you to seek the help of ministers who understand the dark night of the soul, who know how to help people get delivered by God. In the meantime we invite you to pray this prayer of consecration and dedication.

> Father, I pray that by the power of Your love, by the power of Your Spirit, and by the power of Your Word, You will help me to be delivered and set free of the trauma of my past and bring me through this dark night of my soul. I commit myself to love You and pursue You no matter how dark things get because I know that You will bring me out of this and bring forth the humility, tenderness of heart,

and steadfast love that will set me on the mountaintop with You.

Everything I am and have is Yours, Father, and I just want to walk in Your love at all times. I believe by Your Word that I am delivered and set free of all bondage right now through the blood and the name of Jesus Christ. I praise You and thank You that I am *No Longer Bound* by _____. Show me where I need to go to get any more help I need to be delivered and stay delivered. Show me what I am being delivered to, not just what I am being delivered from! Thank You for performing this miracle in my life. In Jesus' name I pray, amen.

Whatever it is that has held you bound, however low you may be feeling, Jesus is right there with you whether you sense Him or not. He was tempted, tried, and tested in everything that you have been. He is able to "sympathize with our weaknesses" (Hebrews 4:15). There isn't anything you have experienced or are feeling now that He hasn't experienced and felt Himself, either on the cross when He took all your sin and sickness or during His walk on earth when He was tempted.

He knows how you feel, and He understands what you are going through!

If you will trust Jesus with just a little of your heart, He will come and begin to comfort you, teach you, and take the pain right out of you. He will expose the lies you have believed about yourself, about others, and about Him because He is the truth. He is the Living Word, and He knows your thoughts, He understands your compulsions and your addictions. He feels your anguish as you can't seem to deal with a troubled marriage, kids who are out of control, financial problems, and nothing ever really satisfying you.

Whatever it is that you are afraid to face or have no idea how to face, Jesus knows all about it. He is putting His hand on your door handle and rattling it to wake you up and incite you to rise up and chase Him! He knows how to heal your heart and lead you through the process of facing it so that you will be *No Longer Bound!*

For Further Help...

If you would like to receive help, we highly recommend a healing week through ministry called Restoring the Foundations. We are pleased to offer this to you at Open Bible Fellowship, Tulsa, Oklahoma. If you are interested, please call the Healing Week Coordinator at Open Bible Fellowship (918) 492-5511. You may mail your inquiry to:

Healing Week Coordinator
Open Bible Fellowship
1439 East 71st Street
Tulsa, OK 74136

Or E-mail your inquiry to:
info@obftulsa.org
Please include:
NAME
ADDRESS
CITY STATE ZIP COUNTRY
PHONE
FAX
E-MAIL

If the Tulsa location is not convenient for you, we recommend you contact Restoring The Foundations ministry at www.RestoringTheFoundations.org. They have ministry teams and training centers in a number of locations throughout the world. They can also help to establish a Restoring The Foundations ministry program in your church.

About the Authors

Joel and Linda Budd have been the senior pastors of Open Bible Fellowship in Tulsa, Oklahoma, for the past twenty-three years. The Budds have pastored for a total of thirty years and have a rich experience in the things of the Spirit. They teach that believers owe the world an encounter with God, and a gospel without power and love is not the gospel that Jesus preached.

The Budds founded and oversee the Firestorm School of Ministry, where believers learn to break off strongholds that hold back confidence, freedom, and anointing. Students learn to discern spirits, lead people in deliverance, heal the sick, and prophesy in the marketplace, at the workplace, and in the local church.

Whether the Budds minister individually or together, the hallmark of their ministry includes physical and emotional healing and deep encounters with the Father's love and power. They partner with and minister in many other churches who are also seeking authentic revival. This relationship network crosses denominational lines, helping emerging leaders walk together in purity of heart and the Father's love and power.

Pastors Joel and Linda live in Tulsa, Oklahoma, with an assortment of pets and two of their three daughters:

Cristin and Haley. Their daughter Joelle is married to David Burris and also lives in Tulsa.

To contact Pastors Joel and Linda
you may write:
Pastors Joel and Linda Budd
Open Bible Fellowship
1439 East 71st Street
Tulsa, OK 74136

or call:
918-492-5511

or e-mail:
lindab@obftulsa.org

Weekly sermons and teaching by Pastors Joel and Linda
are available on the church website:
www.obftulsa.org

Other Materials from Pastors Joel and Linda Budd

Fill Me or Kill Me

Are you desperate for more of God in your life?

Maybe you are crying out like Pastor Joel Budd did when he said, "Fill me or kill me, but don't leave me this way!" Or maybe you are ready to throw in the towel, as Pastor Linda Budd was, unless God moves in your life.

One thing is certain…you are on the right track because nothing much happens without a hunger and thirst for God! That's why Pastors Joel and Linda have written their story. They tell how God answered them in a mighty way that transformed their lives forever and brought them into new dimensions of intimacy, revelation, and power in Him.

Their life-changing journey will challenge you to continue growing spiritually — because there's always more in the Lord!

Soon to be released . . .

So You Want to Date My Daughter?!

With three grown daughters, Pastor Joel Budd gives other parents the benefit of his wisdom and experience in dealing with the issues of dating. This book is the outline he and his wife Linda used for their daughters and those who dated them. If you are wondering how to joyfully and successfully navigate the dating years, this resource is a must. Tested over the years by other grateful dads and moms — and young people — it has gotten rave reviews from parents and kids alike. See for yourself how fun, clear, and clean the dating years can be.

www.ingramcontent.com/pod-product-compliance
Lightning Source LLC
LaVergne TN
LVHW021344080426
835508LV00020B/2107